The Enlightened Real Estate Agent

Buddha's Principles for Success

Table of Contents

Chapter 1. Introduction

Step into a whole new realm of real estate success with "The Enlightened Real Estate Agent: Buddha's Principles for Success." This illuminating Special Report is tailor-made for agents seeking a vibrant balance between professional growth and personal wellness. The concepts explored are inspired by the time-honored wisdom of Buddha's teachings adapted for the modern real estate market. Whether you're nurturing your first property deal or managing a booming portfolio, these principles will serve as a beacon to guide you towards harmonious and prosperous business dealings. By offering a fresh perspective on the real estate industry, this report promises not only an unexpected journey but also practical transformations leading to results that even the shrewdest of agents will appreciate. Get ready to harness the full potential of your capabilities - all it takes is the turning of a page!

Chapter 2. Embracing Change: Transience in Real Estate

The real estate market, much like life, is in a state of constant flux. Nothing remains static, and the landscape transforms with each passing moment. Derived from Buddha's principles, the concept of 'anicca', or impermanence, applies flawlessly to the real estate industry. By acknowledging and embracing this transience, real estate agents can develop a comprehensive perspective that allows them to navigate the business waves effectively.

2.1. Understanding Transience in Real Estate

The first step towards embracing change is understanding transience, recognizing that everything in life, including the real estate industry, is impermanent. All conditions, whether they are positivity and market boom times or adversities like property crashes, are temporary. Seizing opportunities in good times while preparing for the downturns is a crucial aspect of becoming an enlightened real estate agent.

Declining prices can push buyers away, while soaring prices may attract a flurry of activity, only for the cycle to repeat itself in the opposite direction. Prices fluctuate, communities evolve, tax policies change, and client preferences shift with the trends. Accepting these changes and learning to ride the cycle, instead of fearing or resisting it, endows real estate agents with the resilience to remain steadfast amid the industry's unpredictable nature.

2.2. Adaptive Strategies and Transience

Secondly, acknowledging transience helps develop adaptive strategies for a real estate business's growth and stability. Maintaining a flexible approach for different market phases allows agents to thrive irrespective of the market's direction. While the specifics will vary based on the scenario, several key elements remain consistent.

Start by evaluating the current market phase to understand the potential risks and opportunities it presents. Then, set achievable short-term goals that adapt to the identified trends. Finally, be prepared to adjust these strategies as the shifts in the real estate market dictate. With flexibility and resilience built into your business plan, your ability to weather any storm improves.

2.3. Emotional Resilience Amid Change

A key component in embracing transience is emotional resilience. The real estate industry's highs and lows can incite diverse emotions, from euphoria during periods of growth to anxiety in downturns. This emotional rollercoaster can take a toll on an agent's wellbeing.

One of the fundamental principles of Buddhism is non-attachment. In real estate terms, this means not getting overly exhilarated by success or unduly disheartened by failure. By cultivating emotional resilience and maintaining a calm, composed mindset, you position yourself to make rational decisions that contribute to your long-term success.

2.4. Learning from the Past, Living in the Present

To embrace change, one must learn from the past and live in the present. Reflecting on past market trends, consumer behaviors, and successful strategies can provide valuable insights for future prospects. However, while it's crucial to learn from the past, it's equally important not to dwell on it.

The past serves as a base of knowledge, while the present is the battlefield of action. By staying present, agents can spot emerging trends earlier, adapt their strategies more swiftly, and seize new opportunities more readily.

2.5. Accommodating Future Trends

Embracing transience also implies that we must be open to the future. Staying in tune with emerging technologies, shifting client demographics, and future economic and policy trends can provide a competitive advantage.

Whether it's the rise of virtual property tours, or the increased demand for sustainable housing, or the influence of generational shifts on housing demand– keeping an eye on future trends allows enlightened real estate agents to anticipate changes and adapt swiftly.

In conclusion, 'anicca', the principle of impermanence, serves as a powerful guiding force for real estate agents. It encourages resilience, adaptability, emotional steadiness, a focus on present action, and a foresighted approach. By viewing change as an ally and a source of opportunities, agents can achieve remarkable growth and success, fully embracing transience in real estate.

Chapter 3. The Middle Path: Moderation in Investments

As in life, the importance of balance should not be underestimated when investing — particularly in real estate. This chapter, inspired by Buddha's Middle Path, explores the application of the principles of moderation to investments in real estate.

3.1. Understanding Investment Moderation

There is a fine line between investments that prove successful and those that end in failure. Often, the difference lies in the degree of moderation practiced by the investor. Buddha's teachings regarding the Middle Path suggest avoiding extremes; neither hasty risks nor complete inaction bring prosperity. Instead, balance holds the key to success.

To apply this concept of moderation to the real estate industry, one needs to understand what it entails. Investment moderation doesn't imply stagnation. Rather, it refers to a considered, balanced approach to investment; one that doesn't gravitate towards the extremes of over-investing or under-investing. A moderate investor leverages data and diversifies investments, reduces unnecessary risks, leverages the right financial instruments, and factors the current and forecasted real estate market conditions.

3.2. Practice Diversification

Buddha's Middle Path emphasizes avoiding the extremes. Applied within investment strategy, this principle advises against putting all your investment focus on a single property type, location, or renovation strategy. Diversify your portfolio by investing in a variety of property types, across different neighborhoods and market segments.

Match your investment mix to your risk tolerance and goals. If you are looking for more stable returns, a balanced portfolio could include; rental apartments for steady cash flow, mixed-use properties for diversification, and some percentage in REITs, for example.

This approach reduces the risks tied to any single investment. Even if one property performs poorly, others in your portfolio could still continue to perform well, maintaining balance.

3.3. Risk Management

Investing in real estate, irrespective of the market conditions, always carries a degree of risk. Striking a balance between the potential for high returns and the risk associated with each venture is key to maintaining a balanced investment portfolio.

To implement this balance, thorough research and analysis are crucial. Good investors don't gamble; they make calculated decisions based on facts and scenarios. Consider the local economy, market trends, property conditions, and possible unpredictable events like natural disasters.

Also, it's essential to have a plan B: an exit strategy for your investment. This might include options for selling the property or converting it into a rental unit if it doesn't sell on the regular market.

3.4. Financial Flexibility

Often, real estate investments are made with borrowed money. While leverage can provide the opportunity to increase returns, it can also lead to financial distress if not used wisely.

A middle path approach to leverage would be to maintain a balanced debt-to-equity ratio in your portfolio. While taking up credit for new acquisitions, ensure you have enough equity in the portfolio to avoid excessive loan-to-value ratios. This balance reduces financial vulnerability and risk.

3.5. Anticipating Market Cycles

No one can consistently and definitively predict how real estate markets will move. However, understanding that markets are cyclical—proceeding through periods of growth, stagnation, and contraction—can aid in achieving balance with the middle path philosophy.

It can be tempting to invest heavily during a boom. However, moderation advises against such behavior, as it results in overexposure when the market inevitably contracts. Similarly, exercising restraint during market downturns can prevent premature divestment at a loss.

3.6. Formulating an Investment Strategy

Using the advice encapsulated above, the final step of applying the Middle Path to your investments is formulating your investment strategy. This entails determining your risk appetite, setting financial goals, and identifying your investment domains.

Investment strategies should include diversification directives, risk management guidelines, financial leverage levels, and clear benchmarks for reviewing the investment health and performance.

Remember that the Middle Path is fluid, not static. As industries evolve and personal circumstances change, your strategy should also adapt to continue reaping the benefits of balanced investing.

Integrating balance and moderation, as suggested by the Middle Path, into your real estate investment strategy, could be the difference between stagnancy and prosperity. As with all ventures, clinging to extremes can lead to downfall, whereas standing firmly in the center allows you to sway with the winds of change without faltering. Navigate the turmoils of the real estate market with the enlightened guidance of the Middle Path.

Chapter 4. Right Intention: Ethics in Property Dealing

In much of real estate, success is undeniably correlated with intention. Our actions, reactions, and the choices we make inevitably steer the course of our professional journey. Shaping our objectives through the lens of right intention, as suggested by Buddha, can serve as an ethical compass; it can inspire us to conduct our business in a way that not only boosts our profession but also contributes to our sense of fulfillment.

4.1. Ethics in Real Estate: An Introduction

Ethics in the realm of real estate is more than a mere adherence to a set of prescribed rules and regulations. While these exist to provide a basic structure to the industry, genuine ethics refer to the values that underpin our actions. An ethical agent operates from a place of fairness, honesty, and respect, putting the best interests of their clients at the center of their decision-making process.

By practical implication, such an agent doesn't merely pursue deals; they seek fruitful relationships and meaningful transactions that serve the interest of all parties involved. They don't just sell properties; they strive for a synergy between the buyer's dreams, the seller's expectations, and their own professional considerations.

Having a strong ethical framework not only serves to build trust and credibility but also enhances your reputation in the industry, leading to long-term connections and better client relationships.

4.2. Understanding Right Intention in Real Estate

Right intention in Buddhism refers to the mental energy that influences our actions. This is guided by thoughts of renunciation, goodwill, and harmlessness. To apply it to real estate, we should aim to renounce any tactics driven by greed or manipulation, maintain goodwill towards our clients and colleagues, and ensure that our actions cause no harm to others.

This in essence is a commitment to ethical conduct – a way of being sincere and transparent in our actions, fostering trust in our relationships, and doing our best to make decisions that will bring about the greatest good for everyone involved. We can put these principles into practice by:

1. Displaying honesty: Always being truthful about the property's conditions, including potential problems, and providing accurate information about the property's value.

2. Respecting privacy: Maintaining the confidentiality of your clients' information.

3. Acting fairly: Treating each client with fairness regardless of their budget, preferences, or buying capability. Avoid discriminatory practices and strive for an equal opportunity real estate environment.

4. Upholding professional responsibility: Staying informed about current market trends, regulations, and defined standards of practice to ensure that every decision made is legally and ethically sound.

4.3. The Path to Ethical Decision Making

Every day, real estate agents face several decisions. Some are straightforward, but others might test your ethical boundaries. In those challenging times, a well-defined approach to ethical decision-making can be a reliable guide.

A suggested model might have the following steps:

1. Identifying the problem: The first step of ethical decision-making involves understanding the problem's specifics. This includes the parties involved, the legal or transactional issues at hand, and the ethical dimensions of the situation.

2. Generating alternatives: Brainstorm possible ways to resolve the situation. Consider all possible actions and their implications for involved parties.

3. Evaluating alternatives: Evaluate each alternative based on ethical considerations. What are the potential impacts of each decision? Would any decision lead to harm, inequality or unjust consequences?

4. Making the decision: Make your decision after careful consideration. You should be able to justify your choice based on ethical and professional standards.

5. Reflecting on the decision: After making your decision and seeing its outcome, reflect on it. Did it meet the ethical standards you intended? What did you learn from this situation, and what would you do differently next time?

Following this model can allow you to make principled decisions that remain aligned to the right intention and foster a culture of ethical dealings in real estate.

4.4. Cultivating Right Intention

The benefits of right intention in real estate are numerous, but cultivating it requires persistent effort and introspection. Here are several steps to help nurture right intention:

1. Mindfulness: Being mindful of your thoughts, words, and actions can help ensure that you adhere to the principles of right intention.

2. Training and education: Regular training and education about ethical real estate practices can keep you informed and mindful about your professional conduct.

3. Mentorship: Having a mentor or a group of trusted peers can offer support, advice, and guidance in navigating ethical dilemmas.

4. Aligning goals: Ensure your professional goals align with ethical practices. This includes your relationship building strategies, your communication style, and your way of conducting business.

Real estate is a field where you have the power to touch lives significantly. When you act with the right intention, your work can have a profound and positive impact on people's lives. The path of ethical dealings in real estate may not always be the easiest one, but it is rewarding in terms of thriving connections, a well-regarded reputation, and personal fulfillment.

Chapter 5. The Joy of Giving: Building Client Relationships

In the vast expanse of the real estate industry, building rock-solid client relationships is like planting a tree. Water it with care, patience, and genuine empathy, and watch it bear the fruits of trust and loyalty. This chapter reveals the secret to tapping into this much-celebrated principle - 'The Joy of Giving.'

5.1. The Essence of Giving

To truly understand the art of giving, one must first grasp its essence. What does it mean to give and how does it fit into the timeline of a real estate agent-client relationship? In the context of this profession, the concept of giving surpasses the physical aspects to encompass emotional and intellectual giving as well.

5.2. Emotional Giving

Emotional giving speaks volumes in the efforts taken to understand your clients' feelings and empathize with them. This signifies intently listening to their requirements, concerns, fears, and ambitions. It's about offering reassurances during moments of uncertainty and celebrating with them when they've found their dream home. The principles of emotional giving are encapsulated in Buddha's teachings of compassion and empathy.

1. Attune Yourself: Connect with your client's emotions. Try to feel what they feel. Make this emotional attunement your guiding compass in all interactions and negotiations.

2. Be a Pillar of Support: Reassure and rejoice with your clients. Your support can combat the stress and doubts that often accompany real estate dealings.

3. Open Communication: Maintain open channels for honest dialogue. An absolute understanding of your client's needs can only be achieved through continuous conversations.

5.3. Intellectual Giving

Knowledge is power, and sharing this power signifies the magnanimity of a successful real estate agent. This is intellectual giving – lending expertise and advice to assist clients in making smart decisions. Buddha's teachings underline the importance of wisdom and its sharing as a pathway to enlightenment.

1. Expertise Sharing: Extend expertise to clients. Make them understand market trends, legal formalities, investment potential, and inherent risks in each property.

2. Advisor Role: Adopt the role of an advisor. Enlighten your clients on the industry's smallest nuances, enriching their decision-making process.

3. Educational Encounter: Consider each interaction an opportunity to educate your client. Instill confidence by helping them understand, rather than just directing their decisions.

5.4. The Virtuous Cycle of Client Relationship

A real estate agent's success is intrinsically linked to the success of their clients. When you give in the form of emotional support and intellectual advice, you set the wheels of a virtuous cycle in motion. This cycle starts with empathy, leads to improved communication, results in better understanding, and ends with client satisfaction. In turn, satisfied clients mean repeat business, referrals and positive reviews.

5.5. Practical Tips to Building Client Relationships

Incorporating the principles of the 'Joy of Giving' into daily real estate practice manifests as concrete behaviors and actions. Here are some practical steps to follow.

1. Regular Follow-ups: Stay connected even after closing the deal. Check in on how they have settled in the new home and whether they need assistance.

2. Remember Important Dates: Keep track of important events in your clients' lives. Send a small gift, a handwritten note, or a simple message. It shows you care.

3. Be Patient and Understanding: Practice patience. Understand that each client has unique concerns, timelines, and expectations.

4. Maintain Professionalism: Always remain professional, empathetic, and helpful. The trust vested in you is invaluable.

5.6. Conclusion

Buddha's principles teach us that the act of giving, whether emotional or intellectual, can be transformative, with rewards far greater than financial success. It leads to satisfaction, personal growth, and lasting relationships. As real estate agents, employing 'The Joy of Giving' in your practice will lead to a harmonious balance of professional growth and personal wellness, resulting in real estate success.

Chapter 6. Karma in Business: Cause and Effect in Transactions

Unfolding the principle of karmic interplay in a business environment, particularly within the real estate realm, establishes the stage for transformative practices that draw from principles deeply rooted in Buddhism. It views the commercial and property transactions world as an ecosystem, where actions and intentions have direct and indirect effects on the cascade of occurrences.

6.1. The Karmic Principle

The principle of Karma is a fundamental truth in Buddhism, highlighting the cycle of cause and effect that eventually manifests our reality. In its simplest form, good actions result in good outcomes, and negative actions result in negative outcomes. This idea of reciprocity is not merely confined to the spiritual realm but is also prevalent and applicable in the world of business and real estate.

At the heart of the karmic principle is the concept of intent. Intent, being the initiator of any action, carries the energy that determines the nature of its outcomes. Positive intentions often yield favorable results, and negative intentions likely lead to unfavorable outcomes.

6.2. The Rule of Intent in Business Transactions

In the world of real estate, transactions aren't just exchanges of property and funds. They involve complex human dynamics, where intentions profoundly influence the outcomes. Operating from a place of pure and good intent within real estate dealings not only nurtures trust but also promotes meaningful and long-term professional relationships.

Good intent in business is characterized by honesty, transparency, understanding, and compassion; traits, when exercised, tend to create a ripple effect of positivity. An agent offering complete disclosure about a property's related details and flaws enforces trust. A compassionate approach to a client's unique needs fosters understanding and empathy, strengthening connections between the parties involved.

6.3. Karma: A Long-Term Investment

Integrating the philosophy of karma into your business operations is like making a long-term investment. The results might not be instantaneous but the cumulative effect over time is often significant and transformative.

A real estate agent who operates with transparency, respect, and honesty, treating every interaction as an opportunity to sow positive karma, will eventually find their reputation preceding them. This favourable image serves as a magnet, attracting wealth in many forms- tangible and intangible.

Just as a positive feedback loop is created through good karma, so too a negative feedback loop, stemming from dishonesty or malpractice. It's important to remember that the desire for quick success should not encourage business practices that undermine this philosophy.

6.4. The Interplay of Karma in Real Estate Success

When you infuse the karmic principle into your real estate business, every transaction becomes a chance to cultivate good karma, which in the long run, attracts success. Building upon this realization, let's explore how karma plays out in real estate:

1. In property negotiations, when both parties feel valued and understood, it sets the stage for future interactions. Every successful negotiation establishes a foundation for potential referrals, broadening your base and influence.

2. Treating clients with respect and understanding helps to develop deeper connections. These rewarding relationships often usher in repeated business, nurturing business sustainability and growth.

3. Every act of integrity, no matter how seemingly small, contributes to a wholesome image and boosts networking opportunities.

4. Compassion shown towards a struggling client may inspire them to return when their situation improves, cementing loyalty.

5. A transparent approach towards property disclosures, including potential issues, fosters trustworthiness and often leads to successful and quick transactions.

Using such practices, the interplay of cause and effect actuates a thriving environment of respect, transparency, and success.

6.5. Enhancing Karma Through Mindfulness

To become a practitioner of the karmic principle in business, one needs to consciously cultivate mindfulness. Becoming aware of your intentions behind each action will guide the course of your business, invoking a beneficial and conscious cycle of cause and effect.

Bringing mindfulness into play also includes being genuinely empathetic and sensitive to others' needs, fostering open communication, and acting responsibly. Once mindfulness becomes a habit, it acts like a vigilant sentinel, guiding each business transaction towards ethicality and transparency, enhancing the overall karmic imprint.

6.6. Karmic Diligence: A Path to Success

The power of the karmic principle in the real estate business lies in diligent practice and nurturing continuous improvement. Each transaction, negotiation, and interaction offers a landscape to sow the seeds of good karma. Thus, the driving principle of any successful real estate business should be karmic diligence. It's about showing up every day, with integrity and good intent, to carefully sow the seeds of good karma, nurturing an environment that blooms with success, respect, and growth.

In essence, empowering business attitudes with the principles of Karma serves as a constant reminder to act responsibly, empathetically, and ethically, cultivating a prosperous, harmonious, and sustainable business environment in the long run. The insights embedded in Karma provide not just a fascinating theory, but a practical, actionable, and beneficial methodology, a treasure trove of perennial value, a truly enlightened approach to real estate dealings.

Chapter 7. Mindful Negotiations: Mastering the Art of Balance

Successful real estate negotiations require balance. They're a dance between two parties, both with their own desires and priorities. By mastering the art of balance, you put yourself in a position to create deals from a place of harmony rather than conflict. This chapter explores mindfulness principles derived from Buddha's teachings, their application to real estate negotiations, and how to strike a perfect balance for success.

7.1. The Essence of Mindful Negotiations

Mindful negotiation is about being present, attentive, and thoughtful in every moment of the process. It means being in tune with our thoughts, feelings, and emotions, as well as those of the party we are negotiating with. Wisdom from Buddha encourages being fully aware of our actions and thoughts, conscious of how we are impacting others, and mindful of their reactions.

The real estate agent who embraces mindfulness is not just focused on 'winning' the negotiation. They aim to reach a mutually beneficial agreement, respecting the needs and wants of all parties involved. They prioritize understanding over competing, listening over speaking, and cooperating over demanding.

7.2. Mindfulness: More Than Just a Buzzword

For many, the term mindfulness might carry the connotation of a buzzword, a popular term casually thrown around in conversations about wellness or yoga. However, in the context of negotiation, it represents something much deeper. It becomes the touchstone of successful communication, facilitating empathy, understanding, and ultimately, agreement.

Firstly, mindful negotiations require that we elicit and deliver clear communication. Mindfulness ensures that rather than overloading with information, we convey our key points in a crisp and comprehensible manner. On the other hand, while listening, it prevents us from falling into the trap of selective hearing, where we filter out undesirable information.

Secondly, being mindful in negotiation promotes self-awareness. By understanding our own thought processes, emotions, and biases, we can control our reactions better. This understanding reduces the risk of spontaneous, impulsive decisions that could jeopardize the negotiation process.

Lastly, mindfulness fosters empathy, the ability to comprehend the emotions, desires, and views of others. Empathetic real estate agents are better able to understand what the other party truly values in a deal, leading to more effective negotiations that result in outcomes satisfactory to all.

7.3. Principles of Mindful Negotiations

Understanding the practicality of mindfulness in negotiations, let's delve into the principles that form its essence:

1. **Awareness**: The first principle, awareness, calls us to be fully present in every moment of negotiation. We must listen attentively, paying attention to verbal cues, body language, and emotional hints. This increased awareness enhances our understanding of where the other party stands in negotiation.

2. **Acceptance**: As real estate agents, we must accept that every negotiation will present challenges and that all parties involved have their own perspectives and desires. Reflective acceptance, a mindful understanding of reality as it is, allows us to effectively work with these realities instead of against them.

3. **Compassionate intent**: Compassionate intent urges us to treat all involved parties with respect and kindness, regardless of their stance. It is about understanding their situation and fostering empathy.

4. **Non-judgment**: This principle reminds us to keep our biases, preconceptions, and judgments out of the negotiation space. It encourages us to hear all viewpoints without prejudice, promoting equity and fairness.

7.4. Putting Mindfulness into Practice: Steps to Master the Art of Balanced Negotiations

Mindful negotiation is not just about understanding these principles; it involves setting them into action. Here are some steps to cultivate mindfulness in your negotiation strategy:

1. **Preparation - Be clear with your agenda**: Define what you want to achieve from the negotiation. However, keep an open mind, accepting that success doesn't necessarily mean getting everything you wanted.

2. **Observation - Pay attention to details**: During the negotiation,

observe the discourse closely. Pay attention to the language, tone, non-verbal cues, and reaction from the other party.

3. **Mindful Listening - Listen beyond words**: Mindful listening involves not just hearing the words but understanding their unspoken implications and emotions behind them. This deeper understanding equips you with the tools to respond appropriately.

4. **Reflection - Pause and process**: Take some time amid negotiations to reflect on what's been discussed. Make sure you fully comprehend the position of the other party before proceeding.

5. **Artful Responding - Communicate constructively**: When it's your turn to put forth your points, be clear, calm, and collected. Avoid aggressive or defensive language. Instead, use constructive language that invites collaboration.

By adopting these steps and principles, you will find a marked difference in your negotiation abilities. The road to mastering mindful negotiations may be lengthy, but it is undoubtedly rewarding. Through this practice, you are not only securing successful property deals but also cultivating a way of living that champions balance, empathy, and harmony. Embrace the teachings of the Buddha in your professional sphere and experience how mindfulness transforms your path to real estate success.

Chapter 8. Peace in Profit: Cultivating Satisfaction

In the whirlwind of transactions, negotiations, and numbers that characterize the world of real estate, where does one find peace - let alone profit? The answer lies in a journey inward, to the heart of what it means to both serve and thrive in this dynamic field. Buddha's teachings offer invaluable insight into cultivating inner satisfaction, even as you pursue your professional goals.

8.1. The Principles of Peace

Buddha spoke extensively about the nature of peace, the importance of inner harmony, and the practices that help cultivate this serenity. Key among these teachings is the concept of right view. Right view, in the context of real estate, is the ability to see your role not as one of purely profit-driven transactions but of meaningful service. It involves seeing past the numbers and grasping the human aspect of every deal: the dreams, aspirations, and needs of your clients.

Next is right thought: the mindful awareness of your motivations. If your motivation is purely to gain, you might succeed in the short term, but such a single-focused pursuit can lead to burnout. But if you're moved by a sincere wish to serve your clients - to help them find a home, expand their business, or secure their future - not only does work become more fulfilling, but it also tends to be more profitable in the long run.

8.2. Cultivating Peace in the Midst of Chaos

Real estate can be a tumultuous profession. Deals fall through, markets fluctuate, and the pressures of competition can wear even the most committed professionals thin. So how does one cultivate peace amidst this chaos? The answer is mindfulness, a practice of focused attention and awareness advocated by Buddha.

Mindfulness enables you to stay grounded, keeping your thoughts and emotions from spiraling out of control. When a deal doesn't go as planned, don't allow it to disrupt your peace of mind. Instead, use it as an opportunity to learn and grow. Remain mindful of your motives, ensuring they align with the principles of right view and right thought. When the desire for profit threatens to overshadow your commitment to your clients, bring your focus back to service.

8.3. Profit and Satisfaction: Two Sides of the Same Coin

It might seem counterintuitive, but in the world of real estate, peace and profit are two sides of the same coin. It's not a choice between making money and upholding Buddha's teachings. Instead, let these principles guide your professional endeavors, bringing about a vibrant balance between earning a living and creating an impact.

Knowing that your work genuinely helps people can yield deep and enduring satisfaction. You're not just moving properties – you're helping clients make one of the most significant decisions of their lives. Recognize the value in this, and your genuine passion for your job will shine through, attracting clients who want to work with you, and paving the way for financial success.

8.4. Embracing Change: The Only Constant In Real Estate

The real estate market is an ever-changing beast. A profitable property today may not be tomorrow, and what was a buyer's market can quickly morph into a seller's. So where does peace fit into this volatile equation?

Buddha's teachings remind us of the need to embrace impermanence and to find peace in the midst of change. Instead of resisting market fluctuations or getting swept up in the frenzy, strive to maintain an inner equilibrium. Let go of your attachment to specific outcomes, and stay flexible in your strategies.

Importantly, remember that your worth is not tied to the ebb and flow of the market. Continually remind yourself that each deal is a chance to learn, each client a person to serve, and each property a story to tell – this perspective allows peace and profit to coexist.

8.5. Deepening Your Practice

Cultivating peace in a profession defined by profit isn't a one-time event but a daily practice. It is in the daily decisions – in choosing to view your role holistically, to serve clients authentically, and to embrace the constant change – that you fashion an enriching and profitable career.

The journey inward isn't always easy, and at times, it will put you at odds with conventional wisdom. But in the end, the pursuit of inner peace doesn't just serve you. It ripples outward, benefiting your clients, your business, and the industry at large.

Everyday life in real estate is sure to present challenges that test your commitment. But as you deepen your practice, you might find that these challenges pale in the face of the joy and satisfaction that comes from knowing you've made a difference, one property at a time. Such a fulfillment leads not only to peace but also to a prosperous path intertwined with one's dedication and ethics.

With Buddha's teachings at the heart of your transactions, you can traverse the intricate landscape of real estate with greater ease, multiplying not just your profit but also your peace. Remember, the measure of success isn't always in the spectrum of the material gain but widely in the peace garnered in the process. Your profit is very much a product of your inner peace, and cultivating it can usher in a new paradigm of prosperity grounded in satisfaction and goodwill.

Congratulations, the road to becoming an enlightened real estate agent is before you. Every step hereafter, lain with Buddha's principles, promises a trail that leads to success paired with unprecedented inner peace.

Chapter 9. The Wisdom of Patience: Navigating Market Fluctuations

In the fast-paced world of real estate, one may feel the constant pressure to act hastily, to acquire and dispose of properties as quickly as the market bustlingly evolves, as if in a high-stakes race against time. However, just like a well-balanced life, a thriving real estate business involves not just relentless action but also patient waiting, a principle deeply rooted in the teachings of Buddha.

9.1. The Virtue of Patience

Under the Bodhi tree, Buddha once said, "Patience is the greatest prayer." Time indeed holds immense power, and by mastering patience, we can harness this extraordinary force. In real estate, being patient does not simply mean a passive waiting, but a conscious act of electing when to act and when to defer action.

In an ever-fluctuating real estate market, fluctuations can sway in favor or against you. A property that may seem valueless today could burgeon into an immensely profitable investment tomorrow. Also, a lucrative deal at this moment may turn out to be a costly mistake the next day. Thus, patience is an instrumental virtue that helps real estate agents to navigate through these undulations of the market.

9.2. Understanding Market Cycles

To effectively leverage patience, a real estate agent must understand the cyclic nature of the market. A real estate cycle signifies the recurrent ups and downs of the market, typically stretching over years and characterized by four phases - Recovery, Expansion,

Hypersupply, and Recession.

Recognizing these seasons of the market helps agents exercise patience wisely. During the Recovery and Expansion phases, the market is on the upward swing; property prices climb, and demand oversteps supply. Selling during these periods can lead to substantial profits. However, waiting until Hypersupply or Recession may prove to be ill-advised, often resulting in a considerable loss.

9.2.1. Recovery Stage and Patience

Just as the name suggests, the Recovery phase represents the market rebounding from a downturn, characterized by dwindling unemployment rates and steady economic growth. However, despite these positive economic indicators, the recovery in real estate markets usually lags behind. This delay can be disheartening for both seasoned and beginner real estate agents.

Patience during the Recovery stage entails keeping an eye on economic indicators, government policies, and other macroeconomic factors. This is the time for watchful waiting and preparing to make your next move.

9.2.2. Expansion Stage and Patience

Expansion brings with it the promise of increased demand for properties and steady price incline. More buildings, houses, offices come to life as agents and investors act swiftly to capitalize on the growing market. However, patience in this phase can sometimes differentiate success from failure.

Rushing to purchase a property without comprehensive market research and due diligence can lead to financial blunders. Thus, patience at this stage involves careful property vetting and informed decision-making.

9.2.3. Hypersupply Stage and Patience

As the market saturates, construction slows down, and vacancy rates start to climb alongside property prices, signaling Hypersupply. During this time, patience implies strategic selling and renting, so as to maximize profits before the looming recession.

9.2.4. Recession Stage and Patience

Recession presents a roller coaster of emotions for all stakeholders. In this phase, patience means resisting the panic that comes with heightened vacancy rates and falling prices. It entails holding onto properties, prepared to weather the storm until the cycle repeats back to Recovery.

9.3. Acceptance and Non-Attachment

In the face of market fluctuations and uncertainty, Buddha's teaching on acceptance and non-attachment comes into play. Acceptance allows us to perceive market conditions as they are, without bias or fear, fostering better decision-making. Non-attachment, in real estate terms, refers to the ability to disassociate from properties emotionally, thus enabling us to sell or buy objectively.

9.4. Cultivating Patience: Strategies and Techniques

Patience, like any other virtue, can be cultivated. Here are some strategies and techniques to help real estate agents develop patience:

1. Maintain a Long-term Perspective: Keep in mind that property investments are typically long-term. Hence, avoid knee-jerk reactions to short-term market fluctuations.

2. Practice Mindfulness: Regularly practicing mindfulness can help you to stay calm, focused and patient in stressful situations. Thus, enhancing your decision-making ability during market uncertainties.

3. Continuing Education: By consistently learning about market trends, economic indicators, and real estate cycles, real estate agents can gain confidence and patience in managing market fluctuations.

4. Consult Experts: Collaborating with field experts, such as experienced real estate agents, brokers, and economic analysts, can help you make informed decisions.

In conclusion, in the unpredictable labyrinth of real estate, patience woven with wisdom can indeed work wonders. By understanding market cycles, practicing acceptance and non-attachment, and adopting patience-enhancing techniques, you can turn market fluctuations into open avenues for success. This enlightened approach paves the way for not just economic prosperity but also for the peace of mind highly sought-after in the bustling world of real estate. After all, as Buddha once stated, "A jug fills drop by drop."

Chapter 10. From Suffering to Success: Transforming Challenges into Opportunities

In the realm of real estate, as in life, challenges are a given. How we perceive and respond to these challenges often determines our level of success, both personally and professionally. Embracing a perspective derived from Buddha's teachings, we can transform our adversities into opportunities, reframing the idea of 'suffering' to represent not a hardship, but a stepping-stone towards success.

10.1. The Nature of Suffering

Buddha advocated for the understanding that suffering (dukkha) is an inherent part of life. In the parlance of real estate, this suffering could be a challenging client, an unpredictable market, unrealistic expectations, or regulatory hurdles. Initially, these may be seen as obstacles, but once you understand their true nature as not only inevitable but manageable, an evolution begins.

Addressing suffering begins with mindfulness and centeredness—two qualities that promote conscious decision-making. This focused mindset is not about denying the existence of challenges; it serves to bolster resilience, enabling you to calmly navigate turbulence and lead clients towards their real estate goals.

10.2. The Root of Suffering

Buddha proposed that the root of suffering is desire (tanha). In the real estate context, this desire could manifest as the pursuit of high profits, awards, or prestige. While these incentives are not negative in themselves, an unbalanced quest can lead to stress, anxiety, and unhealthy competition.

The solution? Cultivating detachment. This doesn't imply giving up goals but emphasizes the pursuit of objectives without obsessing over results. By focusing on the process, not just the destination, you cultivate patience, tenacity, and adaptability: key ingredients for success in the real estate sector.

10.3. Suffering Can End

Buddha's teachings emphasize that suffering can indeed end (nirodha). This is eminently applicable to real estate, a sphere filled with cycles and flux. No market downturn lasts indefinitely, no difficult negotiation is insurmountable.

This principle encourages real estate agents to stay agile, embracing change as an integral component of the landscape. Maintaining a positive outlook even in seemingly dire circumstances fosters resilience and inspires clients' confidence. It's about acknowledging the temporariness of any challenge and working proactively to maneuver through it.

10.4. The Path that Leads to the End of Suffering

Finally, Buddha delineated a specific path (magga) leading to the cessation of suffering: The Eightfold Path. This offers a series of practices that encourage holistic growth. Following this path allows real estate agents to strike a crucial balance: achieving professional goals while sustaining mental peace and personal growth.

This path asks for Right Understanding, Right Thoughts, Right Speech, Right Action, Right Livelihood, Right Effort, Right Mindfulness, and

Right Concentration. These tenets are productive guideposts that can be integrated into your real estate practice. For instance, maintaining Right Speech during negotiations cultivates trust with clients and professionalism amidst competition. Investing Right Effort ensures your actions consistently align with your goals and values while manifesting integrity in your undertakings.

In conclusion, shifting your perceptions and reactions to challenges—armed with Buddha's teachings—can make adversity less daunting. Through mindfulness, detachment, resilience, and integrity, the path from suffering to success becomes clearer and more achievable. Embrace the journey, and you'll find that each challenge simply paves the way for greater opportunities and success stories in your real estate career.

Chapter 11. Enlightenment in Action: Embodying Buddha's Principles in Real Estate

Buddhist principles have offered guidance and insight on a wide array of life aspects for centuries. With a focus on mindfulness, right conduct, and the elimination of suffering, we can certainly draw parallels to the field of real estate. By embodying these principles, real estate agents can elevate their practice, providing superior service while maintaining personal well-being.

11.1. Mindfulness in Communication

Conveying clear, concise, and honest information is the crux of any fruitful real estate agreement. Buddha underpinned the importance of mindful speech. As an agent, remember that your words can shape and influence decisions. Be thoughtful in your communication, ensuring it's beneficial and void of misguidance.

```
[cols="1,3"]
|===
| Principle
| Application in Real Estate

| Right Speech
| Express yourself truthfully, abstain from slanderous,
harsh, and idle talk.
|===
```

11.2. Maintaining Ethical Standards

Whether aiding in the purchase of a first home or selling a multi-million-dollar estate, the principle of right action can guide ethical decision-making. Making honest disclosures about a property and maintaining professionalism amidst challenging situations can enhance your reputation and longevity in the industry.

```
[cols="1,3"]
|===
| Principle
| Application in Real Estate

| Right Action
| Maintain professionalism, honesty, and integrity in
all transactions.
|===
```

11.3. Cultivating Mindful Awareness

Being aware of the impact your actions have on others forms the principle of right mindfulness. In real estate, this can equate to understanding the responsibilities involved and the implications of your decisions on clients.

```
[cols="1,3"]
|===
| Principle
| Application in Real Estate

| Right Mindfulness
| Be aware of the effects of your actions on customers,
community, and industry.
```

```
|===
```

11.4. Setting Right Career Intentions

Buddhism accentuates the principle of right intention, rooted in the desire to spread goodwill and refrain from causing harm. It's crucial for your intentions to align with the client's best interest rather than acting out of greed or self-interest.

```
[cols="1,3"]
|===
| Principle
| Application in Real Estate

| Right Intention
| Set career goals revolving around client satisfaction
and ethical service.
|===
```

11.5. The Power of Persistence

Buddha's teachings champion right effort or the balanced application of energy in your actions. As a real estate agent, this means persisting through challenges, but also knowing when it's time to step back and reassess.

```
[cols="1,3"]
|===
| Principle
| Application in Real Estate

| Right Effort
```

```
| Give your utmost but avoid overexertion causing
burnout.
|===
```

11.6. Understanding Property and Market Dynamics

Right understanding or wisdom, implies seeing things as they truly are. In real estate, it denotes a comprehensive understanding of the market, the property, and the client's needs and financial situation.

```
[cols="1,3"]
|===
| Principle
| Application in Real Estate

| Right Understanding
| Comprehend the property, market, and client scenario
without bias.
|===
```

11.7. Practicing Calmness and Concentration

Right concentration is about training the mind to focus without getting swayed by distractive thoughts. This can be invaluable for a real estate agent juggling multiple responsibilities.

```
[cols="1,3"]
|===
| Principle
```

Integrating these Buddha principles into your real estate practices can lead to a harmonious and prosperous career, balancing professional growth with personal well-being. Like Buddha's path to enlightenment, it won't be instant, but a gradual transformation towards an enlightened real estate practice.

www.ingramcontent.com/pod-product-compliance
Lightning Source LLC
Chambersburg PA
CBHW071613270726
48661CB00019B/3238